People at play

Bobbie Kalman
Susan Hughes

The In My World Series

Toronto New York
Crabtree Publishing Company

The In My World Series
Created by Bobbie Kalman

Writer:
Susan Hughes

Editor-in-Chief:
Bobbie Kalman

Editors:
Rachel Atlas
Susan Hughes
Lise Gunby

Cover and title page design:
Oksana Ruczenczyn, Leslie Smart and Associates

Design and mechanicals:
Catherine Johnston
Nancy Cook

Illustrations:
Title page by Karen Harrison
Page 30 by Deborah Drew-Brook-Cormack
© Crabtree Publishing Company 1985
Pages 4-31 and cover © Mitchell Beazley Publishers 1982

To Bryn and Griff

Cataloging in Publication Data

Kalman, Bobbie, 1947–
    People at play

(The In my world series)
ISBN 0-86505-069-4 (bound) –
ISBN 0-86505-091-0 (pbk.)

1. Play – Juvenile literature. 2. Recreation –
Juvenile literature. I. Hughes, Susan, 1960–
II. Title. III. Series.

GV174.K34   1986   j790

350 Fifth Avenue
Suite 3308
New York, N.Y. 10118

102 Torbrick Road
Toronto, Ontario
Canada M4J 4Z5

Contents

Ways to play

While I'm at school, I do my best,
But on the weekends, I need a rest
From math and reading and social studies.
Weekends are for playing with my buddies!

There are so many ways we can have fun:
We can skip and jump, cartwheel and run.
We can stand in the field and blow
    dandelion seeds.
We can make grass-stalk whistles and climb
    in the trees.

On a warm, sunny day, we swim in the pool.
We fly our best kites when it's windy and cool.
Sometimes we fish at the end of the pier,
Or go for bike rides when the day is clear.

We can go to the park and whoosh down
    the slides.
We can go to the fair and try all the rides.
We can swing in the Ferris wheel up to the sky
And shoot down the flume with our hands
    held up high!

We can write funny stories or pretend
    that we're cats.
We can do jigsaw puzzles or make pirate hats.
We can have picnics with all of our friends.
There's so much to do – the fun never ends!

Picture talk

When do you play?
What are your favorite activities?
What things do the children in the poem like to do?
Which activities do you like doing with friends?

A sunny, sandbox day

Today is a perfect sandbox day. My friends have come over to play with me. My dad is sitting nearby, reading his newspaper. He loves sunny Sundays, too. We all enjoy being together.

When my friends and I play in the sandbox, we don't always play the same way. Today I decided to build a sand castle. I used my shovel to fill the yellow bucket. I added three towers to my castle. I am putting a flag on top. I want my castle to be the best castle ever!

Robert is using his sieve to make his pile of sand as smooth as powder. He is sifting out all the small pebbles. When he is finished, he is going to put the sand in his dump truck.

Franny thinks it's fun to play without using any tools. She is using her hands to make her own little castle. She likes the gritty feeling of sand on her fingers.

Neil is making lines in the sand with a rake. He likes to mix water with sand and invent new patterns. He likes using his imagination.

My friends and I enjoy ourselves in different ways, but we always have fun when we get together!

Picture talk

What are your favorite ways of having fun? Do you have the most fun alone or with others? How are the children enjoying playing alone and with one another at the same time?

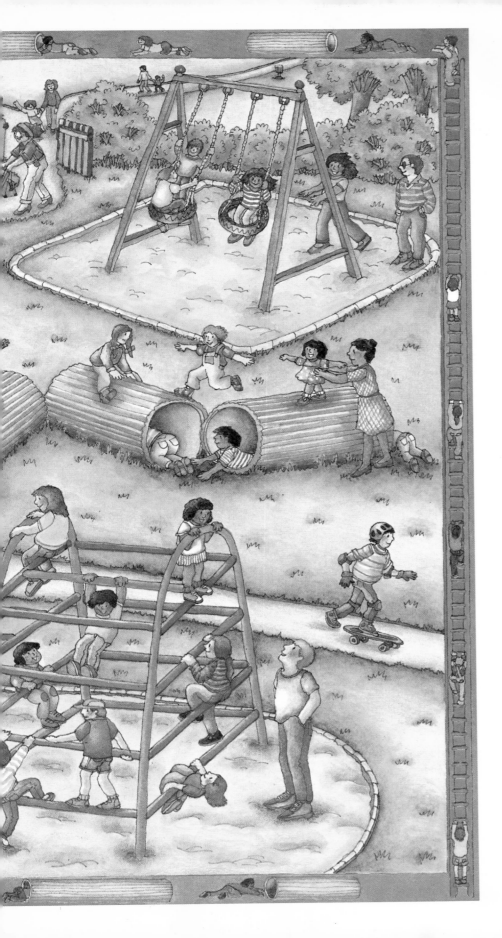

Playing in the park

I live in the city. I do not have a back yard. That is why the park is my favorite place to play. I wonder what I should do first today?

Maybe I'll climb up the stairs to the slide, then I'll sit down, and whoosh ... I'll land in the sand at the bottom.

Maybe I'll go straight to the swings. I'll pump my legs up and down. I can pretend that I'm sailing on the seas or floating in a big balloon.

Maybe I'll monkey around on the jungle gym. I can climb up, over, through, across, in, out, and down, or I can hang upside-down and pretend I'm an opossum!

Maybe I'll teeter-totter way up high, then way down low. I can pretend I'm riding a bumpy camel or a lurching elephant. I can be a baby joey bouncing in my mother kangaroo's pouch.

Maybe I'll play soccer or hide-and-seek. I could ride my tricycle or my skateboard. Maybe I'll rollerskate, skip, hulahoop, or find a friend and talk. Sometimes I like to just sit alone and watch all the people in the park.

What do you think I should do first?

Picture talk
What would you decide to do first? Why?
Reread the story, pointing to each activity named.
Where is your favorite place to play?

9

We like to skate

"Wobble, wobble, wobble. Won't I ever learn to skate well? I feel so awkward. Wobble, wobble, wobble."

"Whoops! I've just fallen on the ice. That ice must be more slippery today than it was the last time I skated!"

"Whee! My scarf is sweeping behind me. My skirt is blowing in the wind. I must hold on tightly to Bryn! This is a fun way to skate!"

"I am pushing a chair along the ice. The chair holds me up while I practice skating. When I get tired, I can sit on the chair and rest!"

"When I skate with Sarah, we are like one person. We have practiced and practiced. We enjoy doing our dancing routine on the ice."

"My friends and I are going faster and faster. I hope they don't 'snap the whip.' I like to skate – not fly!"

Picture talk
Can you identify each speaker? How does each one feel?
Are some skaters more skillful than others? Which ones?
Are the more skillful skaters having more fun than the less skillful skaters?
Do you ever skate? How does it feel?

Let's go swimming

My name is Jevan. I like to swim. I did not like swimming before because I didn't know how. I didn't want to put my face in the water. It made me choke and sputter. I didn't want to try floating because I was sure I would sink!

My parents said it was important that I learn how to swim. They wanted me to be safe near water. They wanted me to have fun in the water. They made me take swimming lessons. I hated those lessons!

First I learned how to put my face in the water and blow bubbles. Then I learned to hold the side of the pool, blow bubbles, and kick my feet. I learned to float. The more lessons I had, the faster I learned. The more I learned, the better I liked swimming. Now my parents can't get me out of the water!

This summer I'm learning to move my arms and kick. I turn my head out of the water to breathe air as I swim. This stroke is called the *front crawl*. Our teacher said that next summer she will teach us to do the *breast stroke*. We will learn to move our legs the way frogs do!

Picture talk

What are some of the children wearing on their arms? Why?
What are the rules at a swimming pool?
Do you think that swimming is fun? Explain.
How does a frog kick its legs?

14

Two ways to ski

In winter I can get around
By gliding over snowy ground.
With skis on my feet and poles in my hands,
I explore the snowy, icy lands.

Many people come to our town during the ski
season. Some of them ski down our huge
mountains. Others prefer to ski on our many
cross-country trails. Both kinds of skiing are
great exercise!

The downhill or *alpine* skiers go to the top of the
mountains on the chair lift. They ski down on
wide, heavy skis. They wear big plastic boots
which hold their ankles steady. They use their
poles to help them make quick, sharp turns.

The cross-country skiers do not ride the ski lifts.
They ski on trails which wind in and out of the
woods. Their skis are longer, thinner, and
lighter than alpine skis. Cross-country skiers
glide quickly along flat ground. They go up
and down small hills, too.

I like both kinds of skiing. I like breathing the
fresh air at the top of the mountain. I love
zooming downhill and leaping over *moguls* or
big bumps. I also like cross-country skiing. I
usually do it with a group of friends. We race
across a meadow or follow animal tracks in the
woods.

When I grow up, I want to be a ski instructor
like my dad. Then I can ski all day long!

15

Fishing in the sea, sea, sea

If I were a fish in the sea, sea, sea,
I'd stay away from me, me, me.

I put a hook on the line, line, line.
One on yours and one on mine, mine, mine.

Then I bait the hook with a
   worm, worm, worm.
(That always makes me squirm,
   squirm, squirm!)

Now over the railing it goes, goes, goes
To tickle the fishies' toes, toes, toes.

I can stand at the edge of the pier, pier, pier,
Looking into the water so clear, clear, clear.

Being out in the air and the sun, sun, sun,
And fishing all day is such fun, fun, fun.

No bites, no fishies do I find, find, find.
Oh well, I don't really mind, mind, mind.

For I don't like the taste of fish, fish, fish.
A good day in the sun is all I wish, wish, wish.

Bass, mackerel, trout, or pike, pike, pike,
It's fishing, not the fish, that I like, like, like!

Picture talk
Point to the people in the picture who have fish
on their lines. How do you think each one feels?
Point to the sleeping fisherman. Tell a story
about what might happen while he sleeps.
Who is catching a big fish? How can you tell?

17

Come fly a kite!

On a windy day, Yuki rushes to the park with her kite. There are many types of kites already flying in the park. Yuki's kite is really four kites which are attached to two strings. The kites have long tails which curl in the wind when they are flying. Can you see Yuki?

To get her kite up in the air, Yuki holds it in one hand and runs with it. She holds the strings in the other hand. Then she slowly lets go of the kite but holds on tightly to the strings. She lets out more and more string and keeps running until the kite is pulled up into the air by the wind. When the kite soars high enough, the wind will keep it up and Yuki can stop running.

Yuki likes seeing all the colorful kites flying in the sky. She loves watching the wind blow the leaves, the grass, and the clouds. She enjoys seeing the swallows play. Swallows are Yuki's favorite birds. She likes the way they soar and dip, and the way their tails look like the letter V. The swallows are having fun on this windy day in the park.

Try this

Pretend you are Yuki. How does it feel to be out on a windy day flying a kite?

Pretend you are a swallow. Tell a story about flying through the park and seeing the colorful kites.

Go to the library and find a book on making kites. Try making a kite. See if it will fly!

Let's dance

Snap your fingers,
Twist your feet.
Wave your arms,
Bebop to the beat.

Wiggle and wobble,
Bubble and hop.
Juggle and jiggle,
Patter and pop.

Every week there is a dance at our community center. My whole family goes. All my friends go, too.

I love to dance! When I hear music, my feet start to tap and my fingers start to snap. I can't sit still for long. I just have to dance.

There are many ways to dance. I dance on my toes in ballet. On Saturday mornings, I am learning to tap, tap, tap. I like to dance slowly or quickly. I like to dance alone or with my friends. I like to make up my own dance steps.

I like all kinds of music. I like music that is soft, but I like music that is loud, too. When the colored lights turn on and off, I sparkle and flash. I like to snap, twist, wave, bebop, twirl, shake, kick, bend, wiggle, wobble, bubble, hop, juggle, jiggle, patter, and pop!

Picture talk
Point to people who are dancing alone, with a partner, and with a group.
Which dancers are wearing the brightest clothes?
Do you like to dance? How do you move when you dance? How do you feel when you dance? Are you taking any dancing lessons? What kind of dancing would you like to learn?

A bicycle race

"Go, Claude! Go!" Jacques yells.
"Faster! Faster!" calls Marie-Louise.

Jacques and Marie-Louise are cheering for their brother, Claude. He is riding in the bicycle race. Jacques and Marie-Louise come to watch all of Claude's races. They enjoy the excitement of seeing the first riders come around the bend in the distance. They watch closely to see if they can see Claude. He is wearing a red, white, and green shirt. Is he one of the leaders?

Claude has worked hard to prepare for this race. He has cycled long distances. He has walked and jogged. He has lifted weights. Claude has worked hard, but he has enjoyed his training. And he loves riding in races!

The cyclists are coming closer. Now Jacques and Marie-Louise can see that Claude is third. The racers will soon be at the finish line.

"Faster, Claude, faster!" shouts Jacques. Claude begins to edge forward. Two cyclists race across the finish line. The flag waves. Who do you think has won the race?

Picture talk
How can we tell that Claude is strong? How do you think his training helped him?
Is being in a race work or play? Explain.
What kinds of races have you been in? Did you enjoy them? Why? Why not?

At the fair

My name is Naomi. I love swimming and dancing. I love skating and singing. But the fair only comes once a year. This makes it a special place to have fun!

As we walk to the fair, I can hear the faint sounds of music and laughter grow louder. I can see the lights grow nearer. I can hardly slow myself down to walk beside my mom.

There's the merry-go-round. It's fun to sit on a horse and grip the pole as we move up and down, around and around. I like the bumper cars, too. They have padding so that no one gets hurt when the cars bump into each other. It's fun to steer the cars and then, bump!

I hear the shrieks from the roller coaster. The train of cars takes the riders along the tracks. They go slowly up, up, up, and then quickly down!

It's fun to slide down the long, winding slide. I like to ride the twirling airplanes. I like playing the games in the booths and buying balloons and candy floss. But I don't like to ride the Ferris wheel. It doesn't go too fast; it goes too high!

Picture talk

What can you see and hear at a fair?
Have you been on rides like the ones in the picture? Was it fun? Why? Why not?
How can you tell these people are having fun?
How are you careful not to get lost when you go places?

25

A special picnic

Yesterday our teacher asked us if we wanted to go on a picnic. You bet we did! Everyone in my class thinks picnics are great. Our teacher thought we should have a special picnic. She asked us to bring a box full of our favorite foods.

Last night, my mom and dad helped me to prepare my picnic box lunch. Dad acted silly and Mom sang as we worked. I didn't know making a lunch could be so much fun!

My friends and I could hardly wait for lunchtime. Our teacher took us for a walk to a field near our school. We cartwheeled and hid in the grass. We played tag and had somersault contests. Then our teacher spread out two cloths. She said, "Would you like to share your lunches with one another today?" What a great idea!

There were a lot of different kinds of food to try. I think I liked the pizza slices and the *taramosalta* best. Taramosalta is a Greek food made of fish eggs, oil, garlic, yogurt, and bread crumbs. It looks like a loaf of brown bread. Can you see it? It's fun to taste different kinds of food. Which new foods have you tasted and really liked?

Picture talk

What kinds of fun did the storyteller have?
See if you can find the Japanese *sushi*. The little sushi cakes are made of raw fish, rice, and seaweed.
What other kinds of food do you see in the picture?

Let's Explore ... Vacations

Most people work hard every day. You work hard learning new skills at school. Your parents work hard earning money for the things your family needs. There are also many jobs that must be done in your home, such as cooking, cleaning, grocery shopping, and laundry. Too much work makes us tired. Too much work makes us unhappy. We must find ways to get away from work and have fun.

Most people work or go to school five days a week. The weekends are like mini vacations. We get a chance to relax on weekends. However, not everyone can take weekends off. Some children go to special schools on Saturdays or Sundays. Some parents must work on weekends. Weekends are often not long enough to give us a good rest from work. A vacation is usually many days away from work. People need vacations.

Spending time together

Families look forward to vacation time when they can have fun together. There are many ways to have vacations. Do you ever have vacations at home, spending time with your family? Do you explore your neighborhood or go to the park with your parents? Maybe your parents take you to the zoo or the museum. Perhaps you go on walks through the countryside together. Vacation time can be a quiet time to get to know your family. Sometimes relatives who live in other cities or countries visit each other during vacation time.

Vacations away from home

The following is a list of popular vacations. Which of these vacations have you had?

- camping trip
- summer camp
- seaside vacation
- sightseeing tour
- visiting relatives
- sports camp
- skiing trip
- visit to a foreign country
- fishing trip
- vacation at a chalet or cottage

How have you spent your time?

Make a list of things you have done during your vacations. Put a star beside your favorite activities. Why are these your favorites? How do you have fun with your parents? If you could go on any trip for your vacation, where would you go? Why? Which is your favorite type of accommodation: hotel, motel, tent, chalet, cottage, boat, condominium, trailer, cabin, your own home? Compare your answers to these questions with your friends' answers. Maybe you can get new ideas for vacation fun!

A secret question

Can you discover what this secret question is? Do not write in this book. Using a pencil, copy the boxes and their numbers onto a piece of paper. Answer the questions listed below by referring to the other pages in this book. Follow the instructions and replace the number in each box with the correct letter.

1	2		3	4	5		6	7	8	9		10	11
12	13	14	15		16	17	18	19		20	21		?

A favorite question

1. Look at pages 4-5. What kind of flowers are the children playing with?
X X X X X X X X X

Put the eighth letter of the word in box 2.

2. Look at pages 6-7. What is floating in the plastic pool with the toy boat?
X X X X

Put the second letter of the word in box 5.

3. Look at pages 8-9. What color of blanket are the picnickers sitting on?
X X X X X X

Put the first letter of the word in box 3 and box 15. Put the fifth letter of the word in box 11.

4. Look at pages 10-11. What are the children on the hill building?
X X X X X X X

Put the fourth letter of the word in box 6. Put the fifth letter of the word in box 20. Put the sixth letter of the word in box 7.

5. Look at pages 12-13. There are four bathing caps in the picture. One of them is green. What color are the other caps?
X X X X X

Put the second letter of the word in box 19. Put the fourth letter of the word in box 18. Put the fifth letter of the word in box 21.

6. Look at pages 14-15. What kind of animal is running through the snow?
X X X

Put the first letter of the word in box 1.

7. Look at pages 16-17. How many boats can you see?
X X X

Put the first letter of the word in box 9. Put the third letter of the word in box 4.

Look at pages 18-19. How many legs does
the caterpillar kite have?

_ X _ X _ X _ X _ X _ X

Put the fourth letter of the word in box 10.
Put the seventh letter of the word in box 8.

Look at pages 20-21. What color are the disc
jockey's glasses?

_ X _ X _ X _ X

Put the third letter of the word in box 14.

10. Look at pages 22-23. What is guarding the
vegetable garden?

_ X _ X _ X _ X _ X _ X _ X _ X

Put the ninth letter of the word in box 16.

11. Look at pages 24-25. What color is the girl's
candy floss?

_ X _ X _ X

Put the second letter of the word in box 17.

12. Look at pages 26-27. What kind of fruit is
rolling out of the bag?

_ X _ X _ X _ X

Put the third letter of the word in box 12.
Put the fourth letter of the word in box 13.

Can you read the secret question now? What is
it asking?

Answers: 1. dandelions; 2. duck; 3. yellow; 4. snowman;
5. white; 6. dog; 7. two; 8. sixteen; 9. black;
10. scarecrow; 11. pink; 12. apple.

The secret question:
DO YOU WANT TO PLAY WITH ME?

Play dictionary

alpine   Having to do with a mountain.

bait   Something put on a hook and used to attract fish so that they may be caught.

bass   Any of various freshwater or saltwater food fishes of North America.

breast stroke   A swimming stroke made while facing down, in which both arms go out in front of the head and then sweep outward and backward.

cartwheel   A sideways handspring in which the body is supported first on one hand and then on the other.

chair lift   A series of chairs suspended on cables and power-driven. Chair lifts carry skiiers to the top of hills or mountains.

chalet   A dwelling built close to hills or mountains where people ski.

condominium   An apartment building in which the apartments are owned, not rented.

cross-country   Across fields or open country.

fair   An event usually held in a region every year with displays of farm and home products, competitions, and entertainment.

flume   A long trough or chute that carries water. People ride in artificial logs down the chute.

front crawl   An overhand swimming stroke in which the legs are kicked rapidly.

grass-stalk whistle   A whistle of two blades of grass placed together between the thumbs and blown.

hula hoop   A hollow plastic hoop kept spinning around a person's waist or hips by the circular movement of the hips.

joey   A young kangaroo.

jog   To move with a slow, steady pace; to run.

mackerel   A food fish of the Atlantic Ocean, related to the tuna, with a silvery body marked in metallic blue on its upper surface.

mogul   A small mound or bump on a ski slope.

motel   A hotel usually found on main roadways. The word motel is a combination of motor and hotel.

pier   A structure built out over the water on pillars and usually used as a landing place for boats and ships.

pike   A large edible freshwater fish with a slender olive-green body, a large snout, and many sharp teeth.

relative   A person related to another by marriage or blood; a family member.

routine   A set part of an act or piece of entertainment.

sieve   A utensil with holes in the bottom used for sifting or separating things.

sightseeing   Visiting places of interest.

ski pole   A thin, long wooden or metal rod with straps and a pointed end.

somersault   A roll in which a person rolls over, heels over head.

snap the whip   A game played by a chain of players who clasp hands and run or skate quickly in a circle. When a high speed is reached, the person at the end of the line or "whip" releases his or her grasp or "snaps the whip."

stroke   One of a series of repeated motions, such as a swimmer's stroke.

swallow   Any of a group of small birds with a slender body, short bill, long pointed wings, and a forked tail.

trout   Any of various freshwater food fish, related to the salmon but smaller.

vacation   A period of time for relaxation and rest away from regular study or work.

23456789   BP   Printed in Canada   43210987